W9-AFS-657

Look What Came From

Australia

by

Kevin Davis

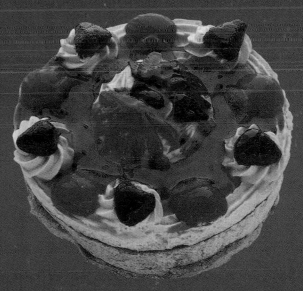

Franklin Watts
A Division of Grolier Publishing
New York London Hong Kong Sydney
Danbury, Connecticut

Series Concept: Shari Joffe
Design: Steve Marton

Library of Congress Cataloging-in-Publication Data

Davis, Kevin A.
  Look What Came From Australia / by Kevin Davis.
    p. cm. — (Look what came from)
  Includes bibliographical references and index.
  Summary: Describes many things that originally came
from Australia, including inventions, sports and games,
food, musical instruments, animals, and words.
  ISBN 0-531-11684-0 (lib. bdg.)   0-531-16433-0 (pbk.)
  1. Australia—Civilization Juvenile literature.
  2. Civilization— Australian influences — Juvenile literature.
  [1. Australia—Civilization. 2. Civilization—Australian
influences.] I. Title. II. Series: Look what came from series.
  DU107.D33   1999
  994—dc21   99-19254
                                                        CIP

Visit Franklin Watts on the Internet at:
http://publishing.grolier.com

Photo credits © : Bill Bachman & Associates: 18 right (Clay Bryce), back cover, 4 bottom right (Susanna Jamieson), 9 right (Penny Tweedie/Galawdjapin), border on pages 2-32, 6 left, 9 left, 14 bottom left, 19 inset, 21 left, 23 left, 25 left, 27 left; Charise Mericle: 5; H. Armstrong Roberts, In 23 bottom right (A. Foley), cover top, 6 right, 26, 27 right (G. Roessler); Liaison Agency Inc.: 21 right (Joan Klatchko), 13 right (Grosset Simon/Spooner); New England Stock Photo: 4 left (Bachmann), 12 left (Mark Newman); Peter Arnold Inc.: 14 right, 18 left (Kelvin Aitken), 16 left (Fred Bavendam), 10 (John Cancalosi); Peter Arnold Inc.: 1, 4 top right, 7 left, 24 top left, 24 bottom left, 25 top right, 25 bottom right (Jean-Paul Ferrero/AUSCAPE), 20 (Michael Jensen/AUSCAPE), cover bottom right (Gerard Lacz), 32 (Guy Lamothe/AUSCAPE), 23 top right (Mike Langford/AUSCAPE), 12 right (D. Leal/AUSCAPE), 24 right (Mike Leonard/AUSCAPE), 13 left (C. Allan Morgan), 19 (D. Parer & E. Parer-Cook/AUSCAPE), 11 left, 14 top left, 15 (Roland Seitre), 7 right (Michael Whitehead/AUSCAPE); Tony Stone Images: 22 (Glen Allison), 3 (Fred Bavendam), 16 right (Paul Chesley), 17 left (William J. Hebert), cover bottom left, 8 (Paul Souders), 17 right (Stuart Westmorland), cover background, 11 right (Art Wolfe).

Contents

Greetings from Australia!

Australian money

Australia is one of the world's seven continents, but it is also a country. It is often called the "land down under" because it is located below the equator. If you look on a globe, you'll see Australia near the bottom. It is south of Asia between the Pacific Ocean and the Indian Ocean. Australia also includes a smaller island called Tasmania.

For thousands of years, Australia was unknown to most people. Explorers from England landed there a little more than 200 years ago. They brought many of their customs and traditions to Australia. They also discovered many great things in Australia.

Some of the world's most amazing animals, birds, and sea life come from Australia. Lots of friendly people also live in this big and beautiful country. Australians like to greet visitors by saying, "G'day mate!" This means "hello, my friend!" So come along, mate, let's take a trip to the land down under and see what comes from there!

The flag of Australia

4

Inventions

Long before European explorers arrived in Australia, native people called **Aboriginals** lived there. The word *Aboriginal* means "the very first." The Aboriginal people have lived in Australia for more than 30,000 years! Originally, they were nomads, which means they did not live in one place for very long. They hunted with spears and clubs and gathered food from the land.

One of the most amazing things the Aboriginals invented was the **boomerang.** The nonreturning boomerang is a curved piece of wood that was used as a weapon in hunting and

Aboriginal man holding a boomerang

Boomerang

6

The Royal Flying Doctors Service at work

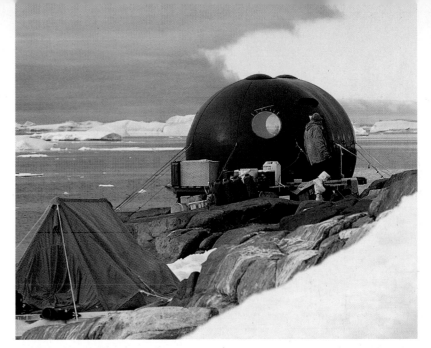

Igloo satellite cabin

warfare. The returning boomerang is a popular children's toy. When you throw it away from you, it whirls around and comes back!

Australia has also been the home of more recent inventions. Australia has lots of desert land, which Australians call the outback. Many Australians live in remote areas of the outback, where it is not easy to get medical care or supplies. In 1928, the **Royal Flying Doctors Service** was created to help people who live far away from cities. Doctors fly to small towns and villages to bring medical attention to people who need emergency care. They can also talk to people by radio to give them medical advice.

The **igloo satellite cabin** is a temporary shelter used by explorers and researchers in the freezing Antarctic. Invented in Tasmania in the 1980s, it can provide safe shelter in both extreme heat and extreme cold. The igloo satellite cabin can easily be transported by helicopter and can be erected by two people in less than an hour!

7

Musical Instruments

Aboriginals have a very old and important tradition called a corroboree. It is a festival, or celebration, that takes place at various times during the year. There is music, singing, dancing, and story telling.

Aboriginal man playing a didgeridoo

One of the instruments used during a corroboree is a beautiful wind instrument called the **didgeridoo.** It is a long, hollow tube made of wood and painted with beautiful designs. The didgeridoo makes an unusual sound when you blow into it.

Another interesting instrument made by Aboriginals is the **bull-roarer.** It is a long, flat piece of wood that has a string attached to it. When you hold the string and twirl it through the air, it makes a howling or roaring sound like an animal! Traditionally, bull-roarers were thought to be very powerful and were used

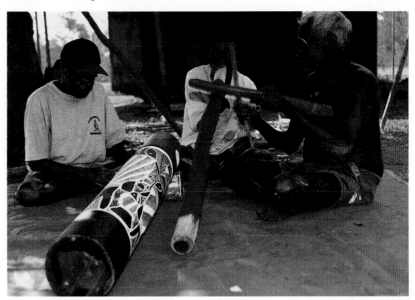

Aboriginals making music with click sticks and a didgeridoo

Aboriginal man painting a didgeridoo

for such purposes as driving away sickness or controlling the weather. It's hard to find a photograph of an Australian bull-roarer. Since it's a sacred object, it's considered wrong to photograph it.

Click sticks are traditional rhythm instruments used by Aboriginals. They are two sticks that are tapped or clicked together. Often, one person will use click sticks while another plays the didgeridoo.

9

Animals

Australia has some of the most incredible animals in the world. It is home to many types of **marsupials,** mammals that have pouches to carry their young. You probably are familiar with the most famous one, the **kangaroo.** Have you ever seen a kangaroo hopping around? They can leap as far as 40 feet (12 m)! Mother kangaroos carry their babies, called joeys, in their pouches. A smaller type of kangaroo is the **wallaby.**

Kangaroo and joey

Wallaby and joey

Wombat

One of the most cuddly-looking animals from Australia is the **koala.** These furry mammals live in trees and spend most of their time eating the leaves of eucalyptus trees.

Koalas are very good at climbing and clinging to tree branches. Young koalas ride on their mothers' backs.

Another animal from Australia is the **wombat.** These are powerful little mammals

Koala and baby

that usually hide during the day. They dig holes in the ground to sleep in and to protect themselves from bigger animals. They come out at night to eat grass.

more animals

Tasmanian devil

Duck-billed platypus

The **Tasmanian devil** is a rare animal that lives on the island of Tasmania. It is a small mammal with black fur and very sharp teeth. It eats other small mammals, birds, and reptiles.

Australia is also home to an unusual mammal that looks sort of like a duck. It's called a **duck-billed platypus.** It has fur and a flat tail like a beaver, but a snout and webbed feet like a duck! The first people who saw the duck-billed platypus were amazed and did not know if it was a bird or mammal.

The **spiny anteater** is another unusual mammal. It has a long, tube-shaped snout. When it sees ants, it shoots out its long and sticky tongue to catch them!

Frill-necked lizard

Spiny anteater

The **frill-necked lizard** lives in the Australian desert. It has a colorful flap of skin around its neck that it can spread into a giant collar. When it is frightened, the lizard uses this collar to make itself look bigger to other animals.

Birds

Emu eggs

Kookaburra

Many interesting birds come from Australia. The **emu** is a huge bird that looks like an ostrich. An emu can grow up to 6 feet (2 m) tall and weigh as much as 120 pounds (54 kg). The emu lays eggs as big as a softball! Although the emu cannot fly, it is very fast. It can run up to 50 miles (80 km) an hour.

The **kookaburra** is another famous bird from Australia. Australians love to hear it sing, because it makes a loud call that sounds like a person laughing! It has a long beak that it uses to catch lizards, snakes, and rodents.

The **lyrebird** is known for its beautiful song and large and colorful tail. It also can imitate the sounds of other birds. When a male lyrebird wants to attract a female, he builds a little mound, spreads out his tail, and sings a long and pretty song.

Emu

Lyrebird

Moray eel and coral in Australia

From the Sea

Aerial view of the Great Barrier Reef

Australia has some of the most amazing sea life in the world. Most of these creatures come from a place called the **Great Barrier Reef.** The reef stretches about 1,200 miles (1,920 km) along the east coast of Australia in the Coral Sea. More than 1,400 different kinds of fish live there!

The Great Barrier Reef is made up of a living thing called **coral,** which comes in beautiful colors and shapes. Coral reefs are formed by tiny sea animals called coral polyps, which form rock-hard skeletons. Fish like to live in and around coral.

The Great Barrier Reef at low tide

Coral and other sea life of the Great Barrier Reef

more from the sea

Scuba divers along the
Great Barrier Reef

Hammerhead shark

Australia's Great Barrier Reef also has more than 100 kinds of sharks! One of the most unusual looking is the **hammerhead shark.** It has a head that really looks like a hammer! Its eyes and nostrils are on each end.

Green turtle laying eggs (inset) and green turtles along the Great Barrier Reef

Another amazing creature from the reef is the **green turtle.** It is one of the biggest turtles in the world, and can weigh up to 300 pounds (135 kg). When it comes time to lay eggs, the mother turtle swims to the shore and lays her eggs in a hole in the sand. When the baby turtles hatch, they find their way back to the sea.

Sports

The national sport of Australia is **Australian Rules Football.** The game was invented about 150 years ago and is a little bit like soccer and rugby. It is played on a large, oval-shaped field. Players kick and pass the ball and try to get a goal. Australians like to call the game **"footie."**

One of the most popular styles of swimming, the **crawl stroke,** was invented in Australia. An Australian man began teaching it to other people about 100 years ago. It was called the "crawl" because people said it looked like you were crawling in the water.

Australian Rules Football

The crawl stroke

Australians love to swim in the ocean. To make sure swimmers are safe, Australians organized the first **surf life savers.** Many people also call them lifeguards. They use surfboards and other equipment to help swimmers in trouble. The surf life savers also have teams that compete in swimming and rescue contests.

Surf life savers conducting a safety demonstration

From the Land

Sheep station in Tasmania

You might be surprised to know there are nearly ten times more sheep than people in Australia! That is because Australia produces more **wool** than any other country. The wool is sold to other countries and then used to make sweaters, pants, and coats. Sheep are also raised to provide lamb, which is a very popular meat in Australia.

Sheep live on ranches that Australians call **stations.** These stations are all over Australia because there is so much open land. Some stations are as big as a million acres.

At sheep stations, the sheep are sheared of their wool (below) and then the wool is sorted and cleaned (right).

Many beautiful gems and precious stones come from Australia, including diamonds, rubies, and colorful **opals.** One of the prettiest is the shiny **black opal,** which is very rare. Opals are usually found in the outback.

Black opals

Food

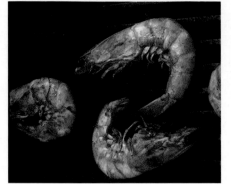

Shrimp on the barbie

Although Australians did not invent the barbecue, cooking on the **"barbie"** is a favorite way to prepare meat and seafood such as shrimp. Australians also love to eat lamb, which is roasted or prepared in a tasty stew.

A very popular food in Australia is the **meat pie,** a small pastry filled with meat and gravy. Australians like to put ketchup, which they call "tomato sauce," on top of their meat pies.

These delicious pies are sold in shops all over the country.

Australians who lived in the outback invented a type of bread called **damper.** This simple bread is made from a dough of flour and water. Australians who camped in the outback baked damper by putting the dough in a cast-iron pot and burying it under the coals of their campfire.

One of the most unusual foods to come from Australia is **Vegemite.** It is a gooey, very salty paste made of yeast. Australians love to spread Vegemite on their bread or use it on sandwiches with butter or cheese.

Meat pie

Vegemite

Pavlova

Damper

A favorite dessert in Australia is **pavlova,** a fluffy and sweet meringue topped with fruit. Australian children also love to eat treats called **lamingtons.** These are small sponge cakes covered with chocolate and shredded coconut.

Lamington

A Craft from Australia

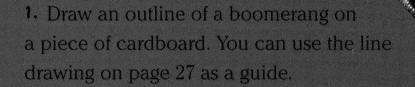

A Boomerang

The returning boomerang, an Aboriginal toy, is now popular around the world. You throw a boomerang in the air and try to catch it as it comes flying back to you. Traditional Australian boomerangs often have many interesting designs painted on them. Here's how to make a simple boomerang yourself!

You'll need:
- Thick cardboard
- Pencil
- Paint
- Magic markers
- Crayons
- Scissors
- Brushes

1. Draw an outline of a boomerang on a piece of cardboard. You can use the line drawing on page 27 as a guide.

2. Cut out the boomerang from the cardboard.

3. Decorate the boomerang with paint, crayons, or markers. You can make any kind of design you like!

4. Go outside and fling your boomerang into the air to see how it works.

5. Make some boomerangs in different sizes and shapes, and see which one flies best.

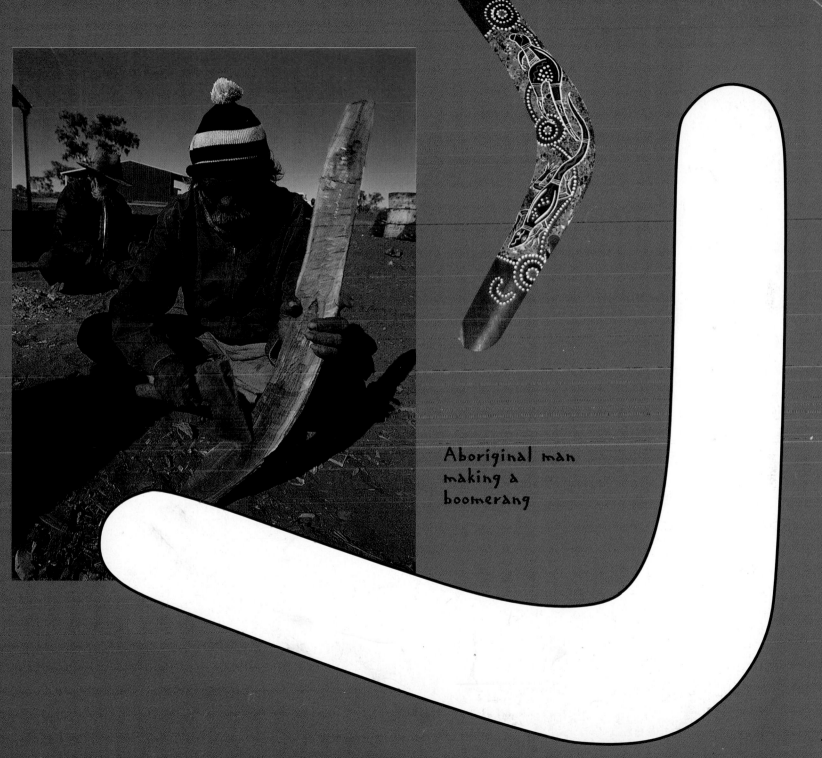

Aboriginal man
making a
boomerang

How do you say....?

People from the United States, Great Britain, and Australia all speak the same language—English. However, Australians and Americans use different words to describe certain everyday things. Here are some examples:

Australia	United States
barbie	barbecue
billy	tin can to boil water for tea
chook	chicken
cobber	friend
eski	cooler
grizzle	to complain
jumper	sweater
knackered	tired
mossie	mosquito
postie	postman
roo	kangaroo
slats	ribs
snags	sausages

To find out more

Here are some other resources to help you learn more about Australia:

Books

Dorian-Smith, Kate. **Australia and Oceania.** Raintree/Steck Vaughn, 1997.

Dorian-Smith, Kate. **Exploration Into Australia.** Silver Burdett Press, 1996.

Dorian-Smith, Kate and Lowe, David. **The Australian Outback and Its People.** Thompson Learning, 1995.

Reynolds, Jane. **Down Under** (Vanishing Cultures series). Harcourt Brace Children's Books, 1992.

Sayre, April Pulley and Koeth, V.A. **Australia.** Twenty First Century Books, 1998.

Telford, Carol and Theodorou, Rod. **Inside a Coral Reef.** Rigby Interactive Library, 1998.

Organizations and Online Sites

Real Australia On Line
http://www.aaa.com.au/online/index.shtml
This is a huge web site with a special kids' section. It has a search engine, links to Australian cities, chat areas, and lists of top Internet sites in Australia.

About Australia
http://www.about-australia.com
A site with lots of travel information, maps, weather, educational information, and cultural facts.

Australian Tourist Commission
http://www.ausie.net.au
Great site with lots of pictures, facts, travel tips, and links to more information about Australia.

This Is Australia
http://springboard.telstra.com.au/australia
Another good jumping-off place to find out more about Australia, with information on culture, education, travel, and lifestyles.

City Net Australia
http://city.net/countries/australia
Lots of maps, tourist information, and links to guides and cities in Australia.

Glossary

aerial viewed from the air

continent one of the major land areas of Earth

equator an imaginary line that divides the Earth in half across the middle

erected built

mammal any of a group of animals that have backbones, are warm-blooded, produce milk for their young, and have hair

marsupial any of a group of mammals whose females carry their undeveloped young in a pouch

meringue a fluffy mixture of egg whites and sugar used in many desserts

pastries baked dough usually filled with fruit, vegetables, or meat

reliable able to be depended on

remote very far away from other places

sacred holy, having religious importance

shelter something that covers or protects from danger or from the weather

temporary occurring for a short time

traditions ways of life handed down from one generation to another

yeast a substance formed by the clumping together of certain tiny fungi

Index

Look what doesn't come from Australia!

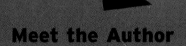

The **slouch hat,** which many people wear in Australia, was really invented in England for British soldiers. It is a wide-brimmed hat with one side turned up. Many people wear

these hats in the outback to shield themselves from the harsh sun. The slouch hat is also the official hat of the Australian Army.

Meet the Author

Kevin Davis is an author and journalist who lives in Chicago. He loves to travel, and Australia is one of his favorite places. This book is dedicated to Kerryn Rainey and her family, who come from the Australian town of Sale, Victoria. Special thanks to Todd and Jo Willis—brave adventurers, tour guides, and friends who live in the outback.